AUNTIE
LOVES YOU SO MUCH!

Copyright © 2020 by Sweetie Baby

ISBN: 9781654077679

My Lovely

_____

Auntie
Loves You
So Much

Look at you,
my small little dear.
When it comes to life,
you have nothing to fear.

Because no matter what, and no matter where. Your Aunt will always find a way to be there.

An Aunt gives a love,
quite different from most.
Our love travels far,
from coast to coast.

If we hear you're in trouble,
we are up on our way!
Aunts can help you,
even on the worst days.

Although days may pass, when I don't see your face. I wish I was there, there is no better place.

And when I do see you,
all the adventures we'll make!
We can play all night,
without taking a break.

And as you grow,
school will start fast.
As an Aunt I'll be there,
for your first day and last.

I'll teach you things,
but you'll teach me too.
That no other love,
can compare to you.

Our love is strong,
because we know it's real.
Once I held you in my arms,
it was all I could feel.

I am your aunt,
and that will never end.
An Aunt's love is where,
you can always depend.

Here is a secret,
something we know is true.
I wouldn't be an Aunt,
if I didn't have you!

You made me an Aunt,
a new name I wear proud.
Because everything's perfect,
when you're around.

Your small little ears,
they hear what I say.
I'll tell you 'I love you'
and that won't go away.

Your small little smile,
it fills my heart with bliss.
And what fixes everything,
is a giant Aunt kiss!

My loveable dear,
so much treasure you hold,
I can't wait to watch,
your story unfold.

And as you grow,
my hand is yours to hold.
Seeing you shine like a star,
will never grow old.

Hugs and kisses,
an Aunt gives them the best.
Just come here for cuddles,
and I'll pass the test.

Because no matter what,
and no matter where.
Your Aunt will always,
find a way to be there.

Manufactured by Amazon.ca
Bolton, ON